Privacy and the Internet

Written by Joshua Hatch

Flying Start
to Literacy®

Contents

Introduction

Have you ever put a sign on your door saying: Keep Out? If so, why? Did you just want to be left alone? Maybe you didn't want others to see what you were doing.

Whatever the reason, your sign meant you wanted some **privacy**. But have you ever thought about what privacy actually is? And what privacy means to you?

Privacy can mean different things to different people. For some, privacy is about being left alone. For others, privacy is about anonymity; that is, people not knowing who you are or what you're doing.

Sometimes, privacy is about keeping secrets. Some people keep a diary in which they write down their innermost thoughts – their hopes, dreams, fears and worries. Many people consider such a diary private and would never want to share it.

But with the advances in digital technology in today's world, is our definition of privacy changing? Is there such a thing as privacy on the Internet?

Chapter 1 Privacy before the Internet

Hundreds of years ago, most people lived on farms or in small towns or villages. They knew the same people their entire lives and rarely met strangers. Many people had little or no personal space. In a small town, everyone knew everyone else. People gossiped, and everyone knew everyone else's business. But this information mostly stayed in the villages and was not spread around the world.

But, even then, people still had **privacy**. Some people wrote their secret thoughts in diaries. Or they had private conversations with friends or doctors or lawyers. They expected these diaries and conversations to stay private and not be shared.

The small village of Hawkshead in England is hundreds of years old.

New technology and privacy

Over time, new technologies meant that less things in people's lives were private. The home telephone is one example.

Before the telephone, conversations took place in person. To keep a conversation private, people just had to make sure nobody could hear them. But on a phone, it was possible for someone to listen in. Also, phone conversations could be recorded without you knowing. Suddenly, a private conversation could be saved and made public without your consent!

The phone book

Everybody had a copy of a book that listed the names, addresses and phone numbers of everyone in town – it was handed out for free! It was called a phone book.

Some people, such as famous people and people who didn't want to be contacted, chose not to be included in the phone book. They considered sharing personal information to be an **invasion** of their privacy. So they asked not to be listed.

Today, phone books aren't common. Most directories are online, but not mobile phone numbers. Many people don't like to share their mobile phone numbers with strangers.

Why do you think that is? Maybe it's because mobile phones are so personal. If a stranger calls you on your mobile phone, how do you feel? Does it seem like an invasion of your privacy?

Chapter 2 Your privacy and social media

Let's say you have some friends over to your house.
Your friends take pictures of you with their phones.
Then your friends upload the photos to social media.
Have your friends invaded your **privacy**? It all depends.
Have you given them permission? What other information
is being shared in those photos? It might be more than
you realise.

Did you know?

Hundreds of millions of photos are shared on the Internet every day. Some estimates say there are more than one trillion photos online. That's more than 100 times the number of humans on Earth. Chances are you are in some of those photos and don't even know it.

Sharing photos online

Photos contain a lot of information. Of course, people can see your face, but they might also see items in your room or house. Maybe they see a computer in the background – something thieves might want to steal.

And there's even more information beyond what's in the image. The photos also record when the pictures were taken, the location and the type of cameras that took them.

When the photos are uploaded, the social media and site might also recognise and **tag** people's faces. That means when other people look at the photos, they can see that other information. They can learn your name, where you live, when you're home and what kind of phones or cameras your friends own. That's a lot of personal information!

Identity theft

Another problem with sharing photos online is that the information in the photos could be combined with other information about you. Maybe you or someone else posted your birthday, school information or the names of your family members online. All that information can be collated.

So what? Well, the more information someone has about you, the easier it is to pretend to be you. Someone pretending to be you could post mean messages about your friends. Your friends might think you wrote them, even though you didn't! This is called identity theft and it's scary!

Identity theft can be much worse than just sending mean or embarrassing messages. If you are an adult and an identity thief gets your name, date of birth and other personal information, they can take out loans, get credit cards or commit other crimes in your name.

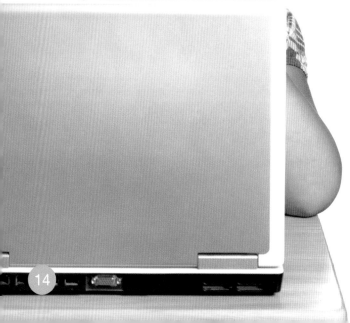

Often, identity theft victims don't know what's happened until banks start demanding tens of thousands of dollars to repay loans the thief took out. It can take years for victims to reclaim their identities. Some never do. That's why it's so important to keep your personal information private.

How to safely dispose of personal information

Think about how you get rid of something, such as a letter, that has your personal details. It has to be thrown out with great care. How do you do this? Not just in the rubbish bin! Shredding documents is a good way to dispose of personal documents.

Chapter 3 Following your online movement

How would you feel if you were in a car and you noticed someone following you? And not only is someone following you, but everything about you is being recorded – the car you're in, the car's license plate number, how long the car waits at stop signs. Would that seem creepy? Would it feel like an **invasion** of your **privacy**?

Did you know?

Cookies are yummy treats, but "cookie" is also an Internet term. Many websites store data about you on your computer. This data is stored in files called cookies.

That's what happens online. When you visit a website, all kinds of information is being recorded. The website knows the kind of phone or computer you use. It knows what other sites you've visited. It knows what you click on, how far you scroll and even where you are in the real world. With everything you do online, a profile of you is being built.

This makes some people uncomfortable. They don't want to be tracked online, just like they don't want to be followed in real life. So why do websites do it?

Why are we tracked online?

Websites track your online activity for two reasons.

One is to make your online experience better. Tracking improves your browsing experience by remembering who you are and what you've checked out. For example, thanks to tracking, the website keeps you from having to log in every time you return.

Tracking also helps sites make money. If you buy a soccer ball online, that purchase is shared with other websites. Those sites think you may be interested in buying other soccer equipment, too. They use that information to show you advertisements for gear like shoes or shin guards. The sites earn money from posting those ads. All thanks to tracking.

Can you keep your browsing activity private?

Sometimes. Many web browsers have a "private" mode, but all that does is stop the computer from recording your activity. The websites and Internet providers still keep track. You can use software called a **virtual private network (VPN)** that tries to hide your browsing by making you anonymous. But that's still no guarantee. It's always possible someone is tracking you online.

Try this
Most web browsers let you see who tracks you online. Ask your parents to check their browser's cookies or tracking data. How many cookies do you count?

Closed-circuit TV (CCTV)

Tracking isn't something that happens only online. Increasingly, technology is being used to track people in the real world, too, using **closed-circuit TV (CCTV)**. In some cities, like London, Beijing and Sydney, there are thousands of CCTV cameras watching people. Many cameras are used to monitor traffic and help officials keep cars moving. But many others are used to see what people are doing.

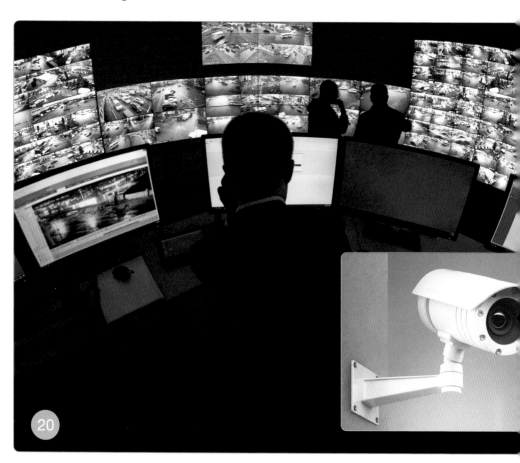

What is facial recognition?

Facial recognition is the ability of computers to analyse a picture and determine if there are human faces in it. Amazingly, computers can even recognise when faces in different images belong to the same person. This "facial recognition" means that the thousands of CCTV cameras in our cities can recognise a person walking down the street.

Some people say the ability of cameras to recognise people means criminals can be spotted more easily, which helps police reduce crime.

But statistics show that cities with more CCTV cameras do not have less crime. Meanwhile, other people say facial recognition cameras erode people's **privacy**. They worry that everything they do is being watched and tracked.

Chapter 4 The Internet never forgets

Have you ever done something you **regret**? Maybe you broke a rule, told a lie or said something mean. Later, you might have felt bad about it and wished you hadn't done it. That's normal. Most of the time, people forgive and forget. You learn from your mistake and life goes on.

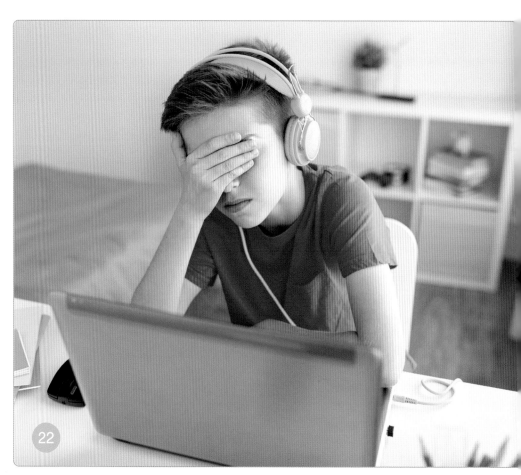

But the Internet can make doing that much harder. When you do something online that you regret, too bad. You might have been in a bad mood at the time and said something mean. But if you posted it online, it's there forever.

The "right to be forgotten"

Forever is a long time. That's why some countries have laws that let people ask to have information removed from the Internet. One law is known as the "right to be forgotten". This rule allows people to request that Internet companies remove information, like a photo or video, they no longer want others to see.

Some people see the right to be forgotten as a way to protect privacy. But should people be allowed to have all their personal information removed from the Internet? What about politicians or celebrities or criminals? Should someone convicted of a crime be able to keep that information off the Internet?

Privacy vs. safety

Sometimes, information should be public, even when some people don't want it to be. If a doctor makes a lot of mistakes and hurts people, isn't that something people should know? Where is the line between the doctor's **privacy** and the public's right to know?

News websites often have to balance when personal information should be withheld and when it's in the public's interest to know. Not everyone will agree on how to strike that balance.

Did you know?

Sometimes famous people use fake names when making hotel reservations. One name you might not recognise is Ingrid Jackson. But if you saw her, you might be surprised. That's the name often used by Beyoncé when she's trying to protect her privacy!

Some people feel strongly about privacy. They don't want anyone to know anything personal, like their date of birth, health information or even their middle name! Other people don't care about privacy. They share everything, including posting selfies online.

As technology has changed, so has the way many people think about privacy. Years ago, people expected their phone numbers to be published in books and shared with others. Today, most people would be uncomfortable with a book full of everyone's phone numbers and addresses.

On the other hand, most people would not like to be followed whenever they go outside for a walk or a drive. But when they go online, everything they do, every site they visit, is tracked and recorded.

Conclusion

Some laws try to protect people's **privacy.** There are laws that prohibit photographing people without their permission. Other laws let you have personal information removed from the Internet. But those laws have exceptions. If you're in a public place, then it is okay for your picture to be taken. If you're a criminal, maybe your information won't be removed from the Internet.

Where do you draw the line on privacy? Are you careful about what you share? When should information be made public? When should it be kept private? What do the people in your family think?

Glossary

closed-circuit TV (CCTV) the use of video cameras to transmit a signal to a specific place; also called video surveillance

invasion intruding on someone without their permission

privacy keeping something hidden or private from others

regret wishing something hadn't happened

tag using facial recognition software to identify a person in a photo

virtual private network (VPN) a private computer network or software that keeps browsing information private from the Internet provider

Index